Walking
My Path

TRUE STORIES OF A
SPIRITUAL LIFE JOURNEY
DESIGNED BY GOD

Nan Beans

ISBN 978-1-64458-321-0 (paperback)
ISBN 978-1-64458-322-7 (digital)

Christian Faith Publishing, Inc.
832 Park Avenue
Meadville, PA 16335
www.christianfaithpublishing.com

Printed in the United States of America

For my beautiful daughter
Barbara
(1957–2012)
who walked her path bravely

Contents

Prologue

Being essentially a very private person, it is with extreme trepidation I set my unusual experiences down in book form to be read by others. So why, one may ask, have I made this choice at all, especially so late in life's journey? In thinking about it, I suppose, it's exactly because it *is* so late in my life's journey. With each passing day I find myself closer and closer to the end of the pathway God has chosen for me on this earth. As the saying goes, it's now or never!

Originally my intention was to leave a chronicle to be read by my children and grandchildren, (and more recently great grandchildren), to open their minds to a greater awareness; there is more to life than the facile things we see and touch. Much more! That is quite important to me... a legacy of sorts... garnered during a lifetime of experiencing the myriad events, which have occurred along my "path."

The work has evolved, however, and I've since come to believe it is intended to be imparted to a greater audience, ergo booklovers everywhere. Why would God give me these curious experiences which I jotted down through my life in notebooks, just to be hidden away never to see the light of day? I believe He is nudging me to share what I've been given, in the hope of illuminating someone else's pathway through life. There is a Higher Power who walks with us and guides us along the way. He hears our prayers and helps us negotiate the many twists and turns of life's challenges if we but ask and have faith.

This is a lesson I've learned over a lifetime, due in large part to the experiences which have happened to *me*. When read by another, however, it certainly wouldn't have the same impact as the actual experiences themselves. But, I draw the curtain back slightly from the mystery that surrounds us, and all I can do is share my stories... leaving the rest to God!

After concluding the book, I fervently hope you will achieve at least a smidgeon of enlightenment or awakening to a "sense of wonder" that wasn't there when you began.

PART I

In the Beginning

There is a master plan to each of our lives designed by an omnipresent and all-powerful Creator, a belief that has been driven home to me over a lifetime of mysterious and unexplainable occurrences.

It isn't anything I was explicitly taught during my childhood years attending the Baptist church Sunday school in my small, closely-knit hometown of Hatboro, Pennsylvania. My mother made absolutely certain I was grounded in the protestant religion. Each and every Sunday, despite inclement weather, she saw to it that I went off to be enlightened in the ways of the Bible. I vividly recall walking together with my best friend and playmate, Dorothy, who lived just down the street. Of course, back in that long-ago time, we were both decked out in our Sunday best. In my case, that meant black patent leather shoes, a little purse, my best dress, and, in wintertime, a small, furry muff complete with zipper pocket that held my collection money.

Baptist was the faith of my father's family for many generations, his ancestors being parishioners at Olde Pennepack Church in Philadelphia, one of the oldest Baptist church congregations in North America founded in 1688, which still stands today. Several of the decayed and weathered tombstones located in the old churchyard mark the remains of both his paternal and maternal families.

Mother herself had been raised a Methodist in Baltimore, Maryland, but I do not believe she subscribed to any specific Protestant creed, although she was a strong believer in Christ. She not only believed—she lived her faith every day. My mother was the kindest, gentlest person I ever knew; and I always wished I could have been more like her.

Unfortunately, she was saddled with me, a more or less spoiled and somewhat rebellious young girl with surplus energy. I was raised an only child during the Depression as my mother, who married late in life, was thirty-eight years old at the time of my birth. I have always felt badly I wasn't all I should have been. But what's the saying, "You can't put an old head on young shoulders?"

Nevertheless, viewed now from the vantage point of a much older and wiser individual, I was very immature even when I married at twenty-two years of age, still a mommy's girl and very far from independent. That independence would come later; and when it did, I was all about it, unfortunately.

Over the next few years, marriage gave me three beautiful daughters to love and care for. I was always very maternal and treasured having my family around me. My husband was a good person, an excellent father, and a steady provider. It was a beautiful life, and I was quite happy and content.

Suddenly, that all changed when I was twenty-nine years of age! My father DIED, and it was a wake-up call, driving me—ready or not, like it or not—from the fantasy world in which I was living into the tangible world. I had never experienced the death of a person close to me. *No*, not *my* father! *Not* John Wayne, the strong, indestructible head of our family. This couldn't happen!

Although he had a heart condition for many years, I was so absorbed in myself and my own life and so completely certain nothing could ever happen to him that I continued living in dreamland and taking life for granted. Looking back, it's hard to believe how totally innocent, naive, and unrealistic I was at that time.

Alas! My father's death changed me completely. I started to question everything about life and felt driven to come up with answers to this, the greatest of all mysteries. And so began an extensive and ardent spiritual quest which continued many years.

I had more or less deviated from the Christian church and became interested in occult sciences and, at one point, visited a renowned astrologer in Philadelphia, who created an astrological chart for me. Briefly stated, I was born at midnight during the time of the new moon, both sun and moon being in Libra at the time of my birth. After reading this and other planets' positions at the time I was born, she stressed how the new moon combination indicated more growth and strength as life unfolds, with many new starts. This certainly has proven correct, and I have grown and matured into a totally different individual through the years—a much better one I fervently hope!

I was hooked and began taking classes to learn more regarding this ancient method of charting the planets on the day of our birth. But not just astrology! That was only the beginning; classes in all types of fringe philosophies appeared on my menu. I was searching for something I couldn't identify, and I felt driven to come up with answers.

My mother, of course, was appalled by this sudden change—appalled by my interest in new-age topics, the study of eastern religions, and questioning the tenets of the traditional Christian background in which I was raised. I put her through much angst back then while trying to "find myself," which I strongly regret to this day.

So, the years passed, and our children grew and were leaving the proverbial nest. My marriage had suffered greatly as I was not the same innocent, dependent little girl my husband had married. Since he was away on business trips for weeks at a time, I was forced to grow up and handle any situation arising in our busy household. After many years of staying home, keeping house, and tending children—which I always loved, by the way—I took a position in a nearby business office to earn money for the girls' college expenses. In other words, I became independent. And I liked it! I liked it very much!

However, there was an extremely high price to be paid. After so very many years as husband and wife, the marriage was more than over. And to this day, I feel the agony and guilt associated with its failure.

These were my most painful and traumatic years, but looking back, I cannot perceive how it could have been different. Rightly or wrongly, I was far from the person I was at twenty-two when I was newly married. That couldn't be changed! I've come to believe it was a portion of my path through life which had evolved over time to create this maelstrom. And I suppose, because of that, I've become a strong believer in destiny.

The events which additionally have led me to this conclusion are set forth in Part II which follows. It consists of many odd stories which I've jotted down in my journal through the years. They are, every one, completely true and without exaggeration. And they all have as a central theme—unexplainable, synchronistic, or "coincidental" events which have occurred during my lifetime. With the exception of two stories ("The Welcoming Spirit" and "Was This a Subconscious Premonition?") all were events I personally experienced. Only because close and trusted relatives related these two interesting stories have I made this concession.

Several of the narrations center around my interest in family history or genealogy, which I have enjoyed as a hobby through these many years. Genealogy saved my life during times of depression and anxiety, giving me a focus and an exciting puzzle to solve. History has always been a love of mine, and researching ancestors back through the ages seems to bring them closer. I heartily believe these long-lost generations desire to be found and their spirits guide me, a feeling shared by other genealogists with whom I've spoken.

These particular stories are grouped together at the end of the book. I've titled this section "Subconscious Communication with Our Ancestors?" as the stories raise, in my mind at least, the possibility of a genuine, albeit subtle, communication with our forebears.

All the stories, which were derived from my old original journal, will cause you to think and question, if nothing else. Some are more amazing than others, some will make you chuckle and shake your head, but all are fascinating narratives that actually happened while walking the path chosen for me by God.

PART II

The Stories

All the days ordained for me
Were written in Your book
Before one of them came to be.

—Psalm 139:16 (NIV)

A Most Impactful Dream

Even though my life has evolved and vast changes have occurred since that day in September 1971, I am still able to clearly recall it as one of the saddest days of my life. Totally unexpected and painful, I feel the emotion yet over forty-five years later.

At nine o'clock that morning, I placed my usual telephone call to my mom before starting the day. I was aware she hadn't been feeling well for a few weeks, but her doctor was unable to find a physical problem. Mother was under a great deal of stress at the time, which we both knew, and I felt this was affecting her. We chatted for a short while, and everything seemed normal. She was in the midst of doing a load of laundry, and I was about to take my daughters to their music lesson a few miles away.

However, only a couple hours had passed before I received a telephone call from my husband informing me that my mother, to whom I was totally devoted, had suffered a massive heart attack and was no longer with us. She was just seventy-seven years of age.

If you have ever lost a loved one suddenly, you will be able to relate to my extreme distress and disbelief. I was in shock, and all the things I should have said or done kept haunting me. But to no avail. It was too late!

My mom and I were exceptionally close. Since I'm an only child and my dad wasn't home much of the time, we developed a very warm, loving relationship. She was not only my mother but a beautiful, kindly spirit, loved by everyone, and my very best friend. I just didn't know how I was going to get along without her presence in my life.

For six months, I continued to cry every day—not gentle sobbing but full-out wailing when no others were around. It felt as though a deep hole had opened in my heart and a large piece of me had been ripped out. And even though others told me I had been a good daughter, I was suffering deep remorse and guilt over things I could and should have done to make her life easier.

And then, one night, I had a very strange, intense dream that my mother and I were floating together through space, both of us attired in flowing white robes. And in the dream, she said only one thing to me—"Nancy, you have to let go."

She had given me her blessing—it was time! So let go I did!

Nevertheless, even now, the dream remains vivid, and just thinking of her brings gentle tears to my eyes. I still miss her terribly, and that will never change! Just one chance to give her an enormous hug and feel her arms around me would be my greatest desire. But that will never be, not in this life!

> *The moving finger writes;*
> *And, having writ,*
> *Moves on: nor all your Piety nor wit*
> *Shall lure it back to cancel*
> *Half a line,*
> *Nor all your Tears wash out a*
> *Word of it.*
> *—Rubaiyát of Omár Khayyám*

A Very Strange 'Dream' Indeed

How many times in your life have you had a dream that actually came true? For myself, I can say... only once! It was during a period of time in the years 1974–1975 when I was undergoing a great deal of emotional trauma in my personal life. I have heard, during periods of high emotion, one is more likely to encounter psychic phenomena. It's possible my state of mind had something to do with the following experience:

When I hopped into bed and turned off the light that night, everything seemed as usual. But as I slept, a strange phenomenon occurred, and a scene unfolded, which placed me outdoors in a somewhat rural area. It was nighttime and relatively dark, although viewing the setting was not hindered by lack of light.

As the scenario developed, I was standing at the bottom of a steep hill, witnessing a huge mudslide sweeping both houses and boulders down the hillside directly toward me. I felt no fear! However, there was a strong sense of not having a physical body around me. Instead, I was witnessing the scene through something other than physical eyes.

Upon awakening, I *knew* it was more than a dream! Immediately, I switched on the TV, expecting to see news coverage about this mudslide. Although I continued watching as I prepared to leave for work, nothing materialized. I *knew*, however, it was an actual event to which I had been a witness.

The term *mudslide* kept going around in my head. In silently talking it over with myself, I questioned why I would see a mudslide!

A mudslide? Really? That's so bizarre! An earthquake would make more sense. My conscious mind was attempting to convince me I didn't see a mudslide, but the term wouldn't leave me.

Being a busy day at work, I had put the dream out of my mind, until I heard the noon newscast coming over the radio reporting a large mudslide which had taken place in California. I was quite taken aback to hear in actuality something I already knew. But in California? Really?

Upon returning home that day, I switched on the television and waited for the evening news with great anticipation. As expected, they broadcast pictures of the devastation from the all-too real mudslide in California I had witnessed the previous night while snuggled asleep at home in my cozy bed.

I've never been able to understand why I would have an intense dream regarding an incident taking place in California that seemingly had no bearing on my life in Pennsylvania. Was this soul travel? Quite possibly. If so, why? Very odd! 'Tis a puzzlement! More questions than answers!

Even today, many years later, if I think about it, I can clearly recall the devastating scene. That's because I *actually* witnessed it!

Up close and personal!

My goal is simple,
it is complete understanding of the universe,
Why it is as it is and why it exists at all.
—Stephen Hawking

Does a Necklace Contain the Energy of Its Owner?

A Fascinating Story That Makes You Think

Is it possible for someone to hold a personal article belonging to another individual and feel the energy emanating from it? There are many people who believe this to be true. This psychic science is called *psychometry*.

I had a very interesting encounter with this process in 1981 as I was attending classes at an adult evening school in the area. The course in which I was registered now escapes me, but during the break, we would meander into the hall to get a cold drink at the water fountain. It was in this way I became friendly with several women from the classroom next to mine who were enrolled in the psychometry class.

At the end of the term, four or five of us thought it would be fun to celebrate the last night of classes at a local restaurant. After choosing a cozy booth and placing our order, one of the girls from the psychometry class, who was reputed to be exceptionally good at this "art," graciously offered to hold personal articles from each of us, to ascertain what impressions she received.

When my turn arrived, I removed a necklace I was wearing and handed it to her without much thought. As she held it in the palm of her hand, a strong sensation of a problem with teeth seemed to emanate from it. She said this was not as serious as I believed and not to worry as it would resolve itself. I laughingly told her that she was way off base—there was no problem with my teeth!

And then suddenly it dawned on me—duh! This necklace wasn't mine at all. It was borrowed from my daughter, Beverly, who at that very moment was home recovering from having four wisdom teeth removed a few days prior.

That same day, she had returned to school and spoken with a fellow student who, at one time, had undergone the same procedure. Upon returning home that afternoon, she was visibly upset as her friend felt she wasn't healing properly after she described her symptoms. Fortunately, time proved there to be no problem, and she continued to heal quite nicely.

The impressions this woman received were truly astonishing since the necklace she was holding did not belong to me. I had mentioned to no one my daughter's wisdom teeth had been extracted, and I was completely unfocused that it wasn't my necklace she held but my daughter's.

So score a *very* big one for the psychometry reader! Wow!

There are more things in heaven and earth, Horatio,
Than are dreamt of in your philosophy.
—Shakespeare, *Hamlet*

A Harrowing Caribbean Adventure

Immediately upon graduating college with a degree in education, my youngest daughter, Beverly, who always had a strong sense of adventure, informed me she, together with a close friend from college, planned to travel to Florida. Seemingly, her friend's uncle owned a large commercial sailboat which he rented out for luxury charters, and their thrill-seeking intention was to sign on to crew for a year or so. Well, okay, sounds like a plan!

I was somewhat leery, as any mother might be, but it turned out to be a wonderful experience for her. Aboard this vessel, not only did she learn to sail, but she actually learned to cook—and cook beautifully—creating gourmet meals for the charter folk who expected quite a bit in the way of food service. (She later turned this asset into a career, working many years for large hotels in Boston.) But I digress.

Eventually, she took a position as chef on a smaller charter sailboat based in St. Thomas, Virgin Islands, when she became involved in a relationship with the captain of this vessel. She obviously was having a great time down there and seemed in no hurry to return home. She was kind and thoughtful enough, however, to invite me to spend a week during the Christmas holidays sailing with them and a couple friends who were fellow sailors. Of course, I said *yes*! Sign me up!

And what a fabulous time it was, visiting these tropical islands I had only heard about but never previously experienced. Now, here I was living the good life, enjoying balmy breezes aboard this beautiful sailboat. Oh, it was just all too lovely! A once-in-a-lifetime dream come true!

For the holidays, the plan was to sail from St. Thomas to St. Barth's, which apparently took quite a few hours, but all in all, an easy sail. Anyway, so they told me! And I must believe it normally is just that.

The cruise went uneventfully the first part of the trip; and I was enjoying the smooth ride, excellent food, and camaraderie of the others. Too fun! It became a much different scenario, however, as night fell. The wind and wave action picked up considerably, and after a few hours we were undergoing quite a harrowing time. This was a squall, the others informed me. My first time sailing... what did I know?

On deck, the waves were breaking over our small boat, soaking us completely, and it was more than a little scary. However, when I went below to escape the water, I felt queasy, in addition to which anything not tied down was slamming back and forth across the cabin floor. Needless to say, this did not inspire great comfort. So I would go topside for a while and return below when I couldn't take it any longer.

And then, something exciting happened—at least I thought so!

While I was on deck, two dolphins made an appearance to the right and slightly ahead of our sailboat. It was quite dark, but the running lights enabled us to see them clearly. They were so beautiful and graceful, diving in and out of rough waves with carefree abandon. The storm didn't bother them in the least; they appeared to be loving it! I was so happy to witness their acrobatics even in the midst of the storm. Oh, thank you, God!

I knew dolphins were reputed to be symbols of protection, so having these two beautiful sea creatures surface
alongside us meant a great deal to me spiritually. I'm not certain the others felt the same, but it was clear to me at least we
were being watched over and all would be well. I personally
took it as a symbol of good fortune. My confidence was high.
I went below, lay down on my bunk, and, with a feeling of
total peace, immediately lapsed into a deep restful sleep.

When I awoke the following morning, the storm had
passed, the skies were blue, and we were sailing into the
enchanting, time-forgotten harbor at St. Barth's. And what a
glorious Christmas Day it was! Three quaintly dressed Santa's
(the French version) were promenading around the docks
celebrating the birth of the Christ Child. Oh, what a picturesque sight to behold! Quite an extraordinary Christmas, one
never to be forgotten! From such as this are memories made!

God moves in mysterious ways
His wonders to perform;
He plants his footsteps in the sea,
And Rides upon the Storm.
—William Cowper

the Reincarnation Game

For many years, I have enjoyed taking classes of various sorts at the adult evening school in our area. However, my favorites are courses in the metaphysical, a subject which has always fascinated me. Sometimes, these classes have resulted in remarkably interesting events unfolding, but none more so than the evening we played *the reincarnation game.*

When the instructor informed us what was planned that night, I was extremely skeptical, as I had no belief in reincarnation at that time. And the game sounded so ludicrous, I almost did not want to participate. Looking back, it was perhaps my traditional Baptist upbringing which was responsible for my narrow-minded approach to the game.

It is played as follows: Each member of the class takes turns exploring their "past incarnations" by sitting upon a table in front of the room while holding a flashlight under their chin pointed upward so the face is illuminated, casting weird shadows on their features. The room is darkened! The other students, we were told, would see changes taking place to the individual; and we were to call out any impressions we observed. Yeah, right! My negative attitude was showing.

And so, we began… and I was quite startled to realize that I, along with the others, was actually witnessing many apparent changes to both facial features and apparel. We read many of the students, but most impressive was a woman who had previously stated she felt herself to have been a Native American in a former life.

She told us she was extremely drawn to them to the extent her home was decorated in an American Indian theme. One would expect, by suggestion, for the face of an American Indian to appear, complete with feathered headdress. That was not the case, however, and a very strange event occurred which made an everlasting impression upon me and I'm certain the other participants in the class.

As her face took on changes, she seemed to have some sort of hat on her head. It took the shape of what appeared to be, as someone called out, a helmet. I *saw this very clearly* and cried out, "It looks like a Roman helmet."

As soon as these words were spoken, she dropped the flashlight and started screaming. Someone quickly turned on the lights, as she was extremely distraught. She then related that immediately upon hearing "a Roman helmet," she had a clear vision of herself as a Roman soldier standing at the foot of a cross!

Needless to say, that ended the reincarnation game as the entire class was visibly upset. I will never forget it as long as I live and still get chills just thinking about it!

> *After all, it is no more surprising to be*
> *Born twice than it is to be born once.*
>
> —*Voltaire*

Do You Believe in Omens?

Do I believe in omens? I certainly did not when I made, what was for me, a rather radical move from my home in Pennsylvania—where I was born and raised—to a new beginning in West Hartford, Connecticut.

In 1984, recently divorced and unable to find a decent-paying job in the area where I was living, I opted to take my daughter Pattie's suggestion to make a move to Connecticut where she was living with her husband. Since they were expecting their first child, this seemed like a splendid idea, as I could help provide a support system for them. I felt excited at the prospect of living in a more stimulating environment as opposed to the rural area where I resided at the time.

To me, this was the big city, and the thought of obtaining a job in downtown Hartford was over-the-top appealing. I had friends telling me not to make the move. "You can't run away from your problems," they said. But I felt it was the right thing to do, and I had the inclination (whether right or wrong), to always listen to my feelings.

Pattie had located an amazingly beautiful apartment for rent in a charming old Victorian building. Right on the bus line, it was large and bright, with huge windows and high ceilings but not available for two months after I was due to relocate. So, temporarily, I rented a smaller, vacant apartment on the second floor of the same building while awaiting the other tenant to vacate.

My son-in-law Bill kindly recruited his brother and a couple friends to help with the move. They filled a large rental truck to capacity with my possessions and made the three-and-a-half-hour drive to Connecticut. How grateful I was for all their help and how badly I felt as we pulled into the driveway of the apartment building and it began to rain. And rain it did!

This was a total downpour worthy of Noah, which lasted the entire time it took to get my furniture and boxes from the truck to the apartment. Immediately upon finishing, the rain stopped as suddenly as it began. I later learned this rainstorm occurred only in that immediate area; a few blocks away, it was totally dry.

It didn't seem possible, and I thought, *I hope it's not an omen that I should not have made this move*, and then immediately dismissed it from my mind as I did not believe in such a thing as an omen.

Even surrounded by unpacked boxes, I was content since I had obtained an excellent position in Hartford, at double the salary I was being paid back home in Pennsylvania. A wonderful job, beautiful new grandson, and only a few days short of moving into my larger apartment—life was good!

And then, shortly after going to bed one night, just as I started to doze off, I heard a sound which I knew was the chain lock on my interior front door being pulled open. Oh my god ! I was extremely afraid as I thought someone was trying to break into my apartment. However, I forced myself out of what felt to be the safety of my warm and cozy bed into the hallway to check and, much to my absolute horror, encountered a large, imposing black man who was already in my apartment and attempting to orient himself in the dark.

The term *frozen with fear* is not an exaggeration, let me tell you, as that is what I was experiencing. I was in total shock, not believing this was actually happening.

"What do you want? Get out, get out!" I managed to yell.

What can I do to make him leave? was the thought that ran through my mind. A strong voice in my head said "*Start to scream*," but I felt extremely foolish as, practical me, had never intentionally screamed in her entire life. The voice in my head persisted urgently, *Scream.*

So, as the intruder advanced toward me, I did scream—and screamed *loudly*—hoping that would frighten him away. But it did not! He kept coming toward me, and to get away, I backed into the bedroom. He followed! Persistently, he came at me, aggressively pushing his hand against my mouth to stop the screaming and told me to shut up.

Still, I did not comply. And as he pushed me, I fell backward onto the bed. By sheer instinct, I pulled my legs up tight against my chest; and as he bent over me, I shoved him with all the might my 120 pounds could muster.

I couldn't believe it, but he was flung across the room and back into the hallway, with me still screaming. He then turned and ran back down the hall, exiting the same second-floor window he had entered off the fire escape. I followed, still screaming as loudly as I could, and watched as he trotted down the alley to flee.

When the West Hartford police officers arrived, they told me the switchboard had lit up from all the phone calls reporting a woman screaming. Seems I was heard blocks away! They alluded to the Kitty Genovese case a few years earlier in New York when no one responded to her screams and she was killed. The officers were grateful the residents in our area were not as reticent to become involved.

Even though it was dark, I was able to give a fairly good description of the intruder; and a witness from another building, alerted by my screams, saw him entering a car parked on the street, which he described to the officers.

The police later informed me this same man had broken into another woman's apartment just a few blocks away that same night and held a razor to her throat. However, she managed to get him to leave by giving him some jewelry and offering him a joint. My daughter later joked that since all I could offer him was a cup of tea, that strategy might not have worked in my case.

I consider myself enormously fortunate to have escaped with merely a couple minor injuries. It could have been so much worse! I have to thank the loud, persistent voice in my head for that blessing. Eventually, the intruder was caught and sent to prison, but it took a long while to recover from this emotionally draining experience. I was unable to sleep in my bed again for several weeks, feeling safer and less vulnerable on the couch.

Thinking back to the "omen," which occurred upon moving into the building, it could only have been a forewarning of the dire incident which was to befall me further down the path. And if that's what the omen signified, I could now put it behind me and move on. I proceeded joyfully into my lovely new apartment where I was quite content for many years.

So if someone should now ask "Do you believe in omens?" my answer would have to be, "Well, I never used to believe in that sort of thing…*but let me tell you about an experience I once had!*"

God is my security guard.

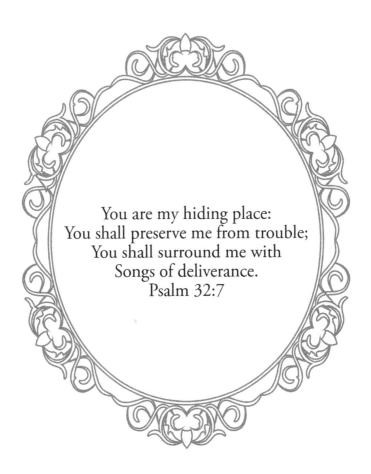

You are my hiding place:
You shall preserve me from trouble;
You shall surround me with
Songs of deliverance.
Psalm 32:7

Today, I Met Erika

A very noteworthy period on my life's path occurred in January 1987. That's the time I first encountered Erika, who was about to become my best friend and closest confidant.

In the months prior to January, feeling alone and unhappy, I prayed God would provide a companion to ease some of the loneliness. There is no question—Erika was the answer to that prayer.

Not long after my prayerful appeal to God, a woman with whom I worked at a large law firm in Hartford, Connecticut, told me about her friend, Erika, who was living with her temporarily since separating from her husband. After many years of being married, she was going through a difficult time adjusting to single life, and my coworker was frustrated, seemingly unable to help her. I immediately said I would be delighted to meet her and attempt to encourage her through the rough spots, since I had been in somewhat the same position at one time. So she happily arranged for us to meet.

From the moment Erika walked through the door of the restaurant where we chose to rendezvous, there was an instant rapport between us. We talked continuously for two hours, never running out of conversation and discovering much that we had in common.

However, it wasn't until she described her journey to America from her home in Teisendorf, Germany, where she was born and grew up, that things became extremely strange. It seems Erika had met and married an American soldier stationed near her hometown in southern Germany. Upon their arrival in America as newlyweds, they moved to Pennsylvania. Since that's where I was from, I asked nonchalantly where in Pennsylvania they had settled.

She replied, "Oh, just a little town that you wouldn't know."

"Well, maybe I would," I said. "Try me!"

"Hatboro," she said.

I literally jumped up from my chair! "No! Are you kidding me? That's where I was born and raised!"

She described the location of the house where they lived, and I immediately realized it was directly across the street from where I resided with my parents as a baby. Unbelievable!

So, to recapitulate, Erika's path brought her from the tiny village of Teisendorf, Germany, to a small town in Pennsylvania, where I just happened to grow up. However, we were not destined to meet until many years later while both were living in Connecticut. It just does not get any more bizarre! It's enough to make you an unmitigated believer in fate!

When we said goodbye in the parking lot, I walked to my car and turned to wave. And guess what? There she was, getting into a white, Nissan Sentra—the same make and color automobile I was driving. I sat with my head hunched over the steering wheel, cracking up with laughter at the "coincidences."

For several years while living in Connecticut, Erika and I spent much time together. Despite later moves (with me returning to Pennsylvania and Erika to St. Louis and Florida), we have stayed in touch constantly and visited frequently. I consider her my very best friend, for now and always…the sister I was never granted by providence.

> *A good friend is like a four-leaf clover,*
> *Hard to find and Lucky to have.*
>
> —*Irish proverb*

The I Ching or Book of Changes

An Interesting Experience

One New Year's Eve, my friend Susan, her teenage daughter, and I, finding ourselves completely alone on this festive holiday, decided to get together at Susan's home for a few refreshments, a glass of wine and an unusual game played by consulting a book entitled *The I Ching* or *Book of Changes*.

I had never played this strange game, not only never played but never heard of. However, I was ready to try something out of the ordinary, especially after an enticing glass of red wine. Susan explained it as an ancient method of Chinese fortune-telling played in the modern age with three pennies.

The *I Ching* consists of sixty-four Chinese hexagrams, each of which contains six broken and/or unbroken lines to which the book assigns meaning. It is all rather complex; but simply put, as you cast the pennies, you put forth a question, which is answered by the way the pennies fall. Each combination of heads and tails has a meaning, which must be looked up in the book of *I Ching*.

Hmm, what question should I ask? Since I had recently purchased a small crystal ball from a nearby new-age shop, perhaps something pertaining to that might elicit an interesting response.

So, after the others had taken a turn, I cast my three pennies and asked the first question. "How can I use my crystal ball to aid in my spiritual growth?" The answer was *effort*, and a dissertation on persevering and I could expect the spiritual growth I was looking for. I was admonished not to let fame go to my head, which seemed totally off base. Where did that come from? At that point, I was somewhat dubious regarding the *I Ching*!

When again my turn came around, the question I posed was, "Will my new grandchild be male or female?" (Needless to say, this was before technology became available to determine a baby's sex during pregnancy.) My daughter was anticipating the birth of her second child shortly, and, of course, I was curious and looked forward to an answer.

But Susan didn't see how it could possibly reply, since the *I Ching* doesn't answer this kind of question. According to her, it is all meant to be taken quite seriously and could not be expected to respond to lighthearted questions. Nevertheless, I stated, if given an answer, then I would believe in the wisdom of the *I Ching*.

Well, incredibly, the *I Ching*, in its response, lectured me for approaching it with such a light and frivolous attitude. Too funny! But it concluded with a sentence that began, "The boy-like contemplation." I could only presume my daughter would be delivering a baby boy.

And she did! In February 1988, much to our great joy, we welcomed a healthy new addition, Kevin Alexander, to the family. Well, all right, Susan, I guess I now believe in the wisdom of the *I Ching*!

This is more of an amusing story than anything, but it's rather interesting how it worked out, isn't it? What is the unseen force or energy supplying the answers to these questions? Too bizarre! But it does make you marvel at the mystery of it all!

> *The most beautiful experience we*
> *can have is the mysterious.*
> *It is the fundamental emotion that stands*
> *at the cradle of true art and true science.*
> *—Albert Einstein, The World as I See It*

An Angel's Wing

As summer 1989 dawned, I impulsively resigned an extremely good position at a major law firm in downtown Hartford, Connecticut, after having worked there since mid-1984. Over the years, I had grown to dislike the job as the firm had grown from a small, friendly office (which I loved) to an extremely large New York–type law firm. It was difficult to tolerate the pressure and cold business practices that seemingly had become part of the position. Basically, I was quite unhappy. So one day, I impetuously gave my notice.

This was not the first time I followed my heart instead of my head, but the economy was far from good. In fact, it was out-and-out dreadful. Steady jobs were hard to come by, and now, I had impulsively resigned a great position.

What was I thinking? I berated myself! I could only concentrate on my obligations, the rental on my beautiful apartment, and numerous other monthly expenses. *Where was I going to find a position at the salary I had just thrown away?* But as tough as this was, I made the decision not to return to the legal field in which I worked for many years, unless I absolutely had no recourse. I felt a deep-down need for complete change.

Knowing I was feeling dejected, my daughter Pattie invited me to join her and my two grandsons for a day at the beach. Of course, I quite eagerly accepted, and it wasn't long before we were sitting on the warm sand at Watch Hill,

Rhode Island, a perfect place to relax and regroup. We were favored with a beautiful, sunny day, a perfect ten!

But instead of enjoying it, what was I doing? Lounging in my beach chair dwelling on my troubles! *Enough of this*, I thought. *Get your mind on happier things.* Determined to get out of this dark mood, I jumped up to join the boys exuberantly playing a few feet away.

They had dug a very large pit, as kids do, scooping out the heavy, wet sand and throwing it on either side of the hole. As I walked around the mound of sand they created, my eye caught sight of what appeared to be an unusual shell lying immediately adjacent. Upon examination, it had the appearance of a small, extremely fragile shell which strongly resembled an angel wing. Amber in color, it measured about two inches long by one inch wide. At the tip, it curled around, forming the top part of the angel wing.

What was this? I was totally astounded! Neither of us had ever come across anything remotely resembling it. We walked the beach attempting to locate something similar but found nothing. Actually, there were few shells on the beach that day, and what we did find were typical large clam shells common to most beaches in the area.

It seemed impossible this delicate shell could have survived fully intact, with the children playing immediately next to it. I couldn't figure it out! Perhaps it was dropped by a bird! It could not have come from the wet hole, as it would have broken, so the mysterious appearance of this shell gave me great pause.

A few days later, with this mystery replaying itself in my head, I paid a visit to West Hartford Library to pour through reference books to identify this puzzling shell I found... or which found me!

I settled myself on the floor in the stacks. There were a great many books on shell identification, way more than I was anticipating. As I looked through each one—and discarded each one—I came finally to the last book.

As I leafed through it—and once again found nothing resembling my angel wing—I closed the book with a sigh of resignation and started to place it back on the shelf. As I did so, a gentleman walked down the aisle close to where I was sitting. In his hand, he carried a rather large book whose spine was facing me. The title jumped out at me, as the first word was written in large, red letters "BELIEVE."

Well, really? Good heavens! Was this the proverbial ton of bricks falling on me? The message was loud and very, very clear—God was in charge! Trust in Him!

To this day, I keep the shell tucked safely away in a special box as a reminder that I'm not alone when problems arise. There is a greater power, unseen, which occasionally gives me a gentle nudge. "You are being watched over." I do *believe*!

By now, I'm certain you may have guessed this story has a joyful conclusion. As doors opened ahead me, I was led to a different profession, a higher salary, and a bright, cheery office with friendly people where I was ever so content. Don't you just love happy endings??

For I know the plans I have for you, declares
the Lord, plans to prosper you and not to harm
you, plans to give you hope and a future.
—Jeremiah 29:11 (NIV)

My Short Venture into Eckankar

While living in West Hartford, Connecticut, each weekday, I walked across the street and boarded the commuter bus into the city. The route directly down Farmington Avenue to my office took about twenty minutes. So easy and convenient! During the commute, we would pass a rambling, old Victorian house with a generous front porch on which was prominently displayed the sign "ECKANKAR."

This is a name with which I was somewhat familiar, as a few years previously I had read a book by Brad Steiger entitled *In my Soul I am Free* which told the story of Paul Twitchell, the founder of Eckankar. The book intrigued me, so naturally, when I saw a place where Eckankar was actually practiced (wake up, girl, you're in the big city now!) I wanted to find out more about this spiritual exercise. So, one evening, I decided to stop by and explore what it had to offer.

It seemed to be a much younger crowd than myself, which didn't make me feel exactly welcome, but I did gather some literature and decided to join a couple of the sessions just to give it a chance.

Eckankar is based in Eastern culture, and meditation is key, being practiced as a group during class or individually by chanting OM, which is a mantra or vibration meant to calm and relax the mind, enabling the participant to ascend to higher astral planes. I must confess, I've never been extremely good at this sort of thing—my mind being too scattered to focus on the task at hand, always thinking of something else I should be doing or planning tomorrow's dinner. I don't have the desire or tenacity to stick with it, so I determined this class was not really for me.

However, during the few sessions while there, I met a young man who had practiced Eckankar for many years and seemingly was able to achieve ascension into the higher spiritual planes. He had a beautiful spirit, and I found myself quite drawn to him. When I related the issues I was having, he invited me and another young woman to join with him for prayer and meditation in a smaller, more intimate setting outside the main area.

And it was in that silent, dim little room where a wonderful experience occurred, the thought of which remains with me. The three of us were there but a few minutes focusing on the OM chant when I developed an awareness of an indescribable sense of *absolute love* pervading the room, seeming to drift down from above and become an all-encompassing cloud infusing my being.

Afterward, the others said they felt it also, but I don't believe they could have; they were much too complacent. I, myself, was awestruck! For almost three days, this veil of love enveloped me before gradually dissipating. It was a *most* breathtaking sensation.

I was never able to duplicate the experience, even after attending more sessions. Apparently, it was one and done! However, I was blessed to have received this amazing token of God's love at all. It is not bestowed on everyone! Thank you, God.

Having been the recipient of this astonishingly beautiful gift, I passionately believe I will feel God's *absolute love* once again encircling me when life on this earthly plane has ended.

Oh, I surely do hope so!

God is Love.

Angels to the Rescue

June 8, 1996, began just like any other Saturday. Upon awakening that beautiful spring morning, I was excited to check out tag sales in the area (garage sales or yard sales elsewhere) of which there are many in West Hartford, Connecticut. This area of lovely older homes was alive with busy residents cleaning out and throwing out in springtime—exactly the sort of place to discover good buys. So, having a great morning to look forward to, I stepped into the shower.

And at that moment, an *incredibly* strange thing happened! Issuing from my mouth, *unbidden* and *explosive*, came a *deep, loud*, compellingly strong voice, reciting a morning mantra which I had spoken every morning for years but had neglected the past several months:

> *I am surrounded by the white light of*
> *God's protection, where no evil can enter,*
> *and I will send forth no evil.*

This was *not* my voice! Not even close! And the thought of saying this never crossed my mind! I was so startled that I uttered aloud, "Oh my god! Where did that come from?" It was beyond strange, but I continued my morning routine, anxious to get out early and find the bargains.

After stopping at a couple promising sales but finding nothing, I unknowingly drove into an intersection through a red light while focusing on a tag sale sign posted on the tele-phone pole. Stupid me! Immediately, my car was rammed on the passenger side by another vehicle. I heard myself scream-ing as the impact lifted my automobile into the air and turned it over, bringing it to rest on the roof. My seatbelt was fastened fortunately, or I would have been summarily tossed through the open sunroof.

The roof of the car was completely smashed, but I was able to slither out the driver's window through shattered glass and walk away pretty much unscathed, except for a small glass cut. The other driver was also uninjured, but my car was totaled and towed from the scene. An eyewitness recounted never seeing anything like it. From her perspective, the car floated down in slow motion, "like a feather."

Well, let me tell you, this was extremely upsetting! I had never had an accident in my life, and now here I was involved in a rollover, which was *my* fault. Upon coming to get me, my daughter arrived before the car was up righted, a traumatic sight indeed. I spent the rest of the day at her home trying to recover emotionally; but that evening, feeling some-what calmed down, I asked her to drive me home.

As we walked into my living room, we both gasped in unison! Hundreds of fragments scattered about the floor were all that remained of a beautiful white ceramic angel which, for years, had graced a table under the front window. I can only assume a gust of wind came blowing through and hurled the statue to the floor.

And that, folks, is the practical explanation. But in my deepest being, I am confident it goes well beyond that. The angel, whose voice came through me that morning, protected me from danger and chose to leave a strong message to that effect which could hardly be ignored.

The most astonishing experience of my life, by far!

For he shall give his angels charge over thee,
To keep thee in all thy ways.
They shall bear thee up in their hands, lest thou
dash thy foot against a stone.

—Psalm 91: 11–12

Exploring Psychic Readings

While perusing a list of educational classes available locally, I jumped at the opportunity of joining a session called "Exploring the Psychic Dimension" taught by a professor from Cambridge University.

Delving into the world of psychic phenomena has always drawn me like a magnet, and joining this class could be the perfect opportunity to experience something unique and different. Being unsure what to expect, it was with mixed feelings I learned we would be practicing psychic readings on other class members. I felt totally incompetent but thought I'd give it a go. (What choice did I have? I was there.)

After basic instruction, the professor had the class pair off, and I practiced psychically reading a few individuals in the class with moderate success. In one instance, I envisioned a woman wearing a red coat, which she told me she had recently purchased. However, I remained unconvinced. What I did ascertain could be attributed to good guesswork and believed my psychic abilities remained wanting.

However, there was one young girl named Mary Beth, who stands out in my mind. I began by taking hold of her hands, thinking my impressions might be stronger. Good instinct! From the moment we touched, I could feel severe depression bringing me to the brink of tears. I told her she was a gentle, sensitive individual looking for answers, but she had suffered a loss involving a man. (Not sure that thought was intuition! Isn't that usually the case?) She pronounced me right on all counts. Again, the uncertainty! Was this intuition or merely conjecture?

Nonetheless, the oddity of my experience with Mary Beth was not the psychic reading itself but the transfer of intense energy passing between us. One could feel her physically relaxing and tensions draining away. Unfortunately, I was the recipient of the sadness she was releasing. At the conclusion of the session, she felt *so* much better. On the other hand, I felt *so* much worse. An interesting experience!

> *There are energies in each atom,*
> *even of the physical body,*
> *That are the shadows of the whole universe.*
> —*Edgar Cayce,*
> *Reading 633-2*

The Power of Faith

Still living in West Hartford, Connecticut, in 1997 but speedily approaching my retirement, I felt an overwhelming desire to return to my Pennsylvania roots. My son-in-law's career had already moved their family back to that area, which worked out well for me. Therefore, as much as I enjoyed my many years in New England, it was time to move on. I found myself becoming *so* excited! Goodbye, Connecticut! Hello, Pennsylvania! Get ready... I'm on my way!

My long-term plan was to devote the free time retirement provided to my passion, genealogy. Accordingly, I wanted to find an old dwelling that exuded the ambiance of a bygone era to better enable me to emotionally connect to those ancestors veiled by time. Since residing in an early Bucks County stone farmhouse had always been one of my fondest desires, I began praying for God to lead me to a lovely old place, fitting this description but with affordable rent (a difficult combination to come by).

There were several requirements on my list, however. In addition to taking my gorgeous Maine Coon cat, Miss Martha, I was desirous of a peaceful environment, with wildlife abounding, surrounded by old trees, and plentiful open spaces to garden (and all this on a limited budget, mind you!). It was an extensive wish list, but if God answers prayer, why not this one?

My desk at work became a gallery of bucolic scenes from Bucks County with its picturesque old barns, fieldstone walls, and historic homes. I totally immersed myself in positive thoughts and prayers, imploring God to lead me to the perfect place.

Meanwhile, at her home in Pennsylvania, my daughter Pattie was being helpful, checking real estate ads, but with only a month to go and nothing coming along, I was feeling family pressure that I had set my sights too high and should settle for less. I still had a deep belief, however, there was a place meant just for me, and I must continue to believe in God's promise. After all, didn't the Bible tell us in Philippians 4:6, "Be anxious for nothing, but in everything by prayer and supplication, with thanksgiving, let your requests be made known to God?" I had done just that. Now I needed to wait for Him to come through.

With only three weeks until the scheduled move, I received a telephone call from Pattie with discouraging news. There were no listings in the paper worthy of a response. Getting somewhat annoyed at what I felt to be her negative attitude, I emphatically instructed her to "look in the boxes" surrounding the classified columns. I just knew it was there; God would not let me down!

"Oh, Mom, here's an ad placed by a real estate agency—'old carriage house, will exchange work for rent.'"

"That's the one, Pattie. Please call it."

I had a deep knowing this was the place God had chosen for me.

And it was! As ordered...one old stone carriage house for Miss Martha and myself; located on a beautiful, sprawling estate of 120 acres, with ponds, barns, and walking trails where I could pick berries, garden, and enjoy nature. Absolutely perfect!

By way of confirmation, God decided the time was right to deliver a message on moving day as I excitedly turned into the long tree-lined driveway leading to my new home. Just to let me know He was "somewhat" involved, the song playing on the car radio was one of my favorite old hymns "Great Is Thy Faithfulness." Beautiful!

Thank you, God, for prayers answered and blessings provided!

"Every good gift and every perfect gift is from above, and comes down from the Father of lights, with whom there is no variation or shadow of turning."
—James 1:17 (KJV)

Great Is Thy Faithfulness

Music—Thomas O. Chisholm
Lyrics—William M. Runyan

Great is Thy faithfulness, O God my Father!
There is no shadow of turning with Thee;
Thou changest not, Thy compassions, they fail not:
As Thou hast been Thou forever wilt be.

Chorus

Great is Thy faithfulness! Great is Thy faithfulness!
Morning by morning new mercies I see;
All I have needed Thy hand hath provided
Great is Thy faithfulness, Lord, unto me!

Summer and winter, and springtime and harvest,
Sun, moon and stars in their courses above,
Join with all nature in manifold witness
To Thy great faithfulness, mercy and love.

Pardon for sin and a peace that endureth,
Thine own dear presence to cheer and to guide,
Strength for today and bright hope for tomorrow
Blessings all mine, with ten thousand beside!

Shared Experiences

The year 1998 found me retired and working part time in a large gift shop in Peddler's Village, a tourist destination of lovely shops and restaurants in beautiful, bucolic Bucks County, Pennsylvania. And it was there I met and became friends with Donna.

As we worked together, we chatted, realizing both of us grew up in Hatboro, a little town about fifteen miles distant. When she mentioned her maiden name, I immediately asked if she had an older brother, Steve, whom I had known back in the day. Yes, she replied, they had both attended my high school, although Donna was quite a few years younger. When I laughingly told her the house my family bought in 1949 was purchased from her parents, we started to giggle. And, as it turned out, both Donna and I had occupied the same bedroom in that home. Too funny!

Over time, it came to light we shared something more in common. Many years earlier, I was employed at a small manufacturing company, having left in 1957 to start a family. As I departed, Donna obtained a position in the small department I was leaving. Actually, we realized she took the job of the woman who replaced me. Even though we never met back then, we knew many of the same people from over forty years ago.

We both found this pretty humorous and laughed about the strangeness of it all. Strange, but not eerie! Eerie was still on the way!

Sometime later, upon nonchalantly asking Donna where she and her husband lived, her answer triggered goosebumps! The location of her home in an out-of-the-way rural setting, together with a description of the house, sounded strikingly similar to a residence my father wanted to purchase from his friend, the builder, many years earlier. I was stunned! What are the chances?

Together with my mom and dad, I had been there many times while it was under construction. We were excited to possibly move to our dream home. Sadly, that was not to be. In my memory, however, I recalled fantasizing about a wonderful second-floor bedroom with a balcony I had staked out for my very own. Seemed so romantic to a teenage girl.

Holding my breath, I asked incredulously, "Does it have a balcony, Donna?" And just what do you think she answered?

Visiting Donna's home for the first time was rather emotional, to say the least. Tearfully walking up her front path, I wistfully reflected on those long-ago days when my parents were alive and dreaming of becoming new homeowners. And now, here I was again many years later, coming full circle.

Life is indeed strange!

That's too coincidental to be a coincidence.
—*Yogi Berra*

The Bluebird of Happiness

I had never seen a bluebird. Even though I enjoy watching a vast variety of birds gathering around my feeders and nesting boxes, this was one species that continued to elude me. The closest I came to a sighting was on a visit to my friend, Erika's home in Missouri, the state which named the eastern bluebird it's official state bird.

As we left the airport, a bird flew across our windshield, just a few feet in front of us. We both thought it was a bluebird but could not be sure, as it happened so suddenly. I remarked that bluebirds were a good-luck sign, and the sighting was predicting we would have a wonderful time during this visit (which we did). I was disappointed, though, not to have a definite sighting to add to my Life List.

My search for bluebirds, however, was not necessarily the variety found in my tattered and well-used copy of Roger Tory Peterson's *Field Guide to the Birds*. For several years, I had scoured flea markets and antique shops in a never-ending quest for three old chalk-ware bluebirds.

At one time, my youngest daughter, Beverly, had purchased a set in an old antique shop in Massachusetts and arranged them in flight along a wall of her apartment in Boston where she had taken up residence. They added a cheerful touch, and she was quite fond of them. Sadly, they were lost during many moves and never replaced. So it had become somewhat of a joke between us that I was always keeping an eye out for her bluebirds during my flea market visits.

Beverly eventually married and gave birth to a healthy son, Ryan. She and her family settled in the Boston area, so I did not see her regularly, though we kept in touch frequently by phone.

The years flew by, and with their son getting older, Beverly and her husband yearned to have another child but suffered three miscarriages in the attempt. This was extremely traumatic to Beverly especially, who put herself under a specialist's care hoping to retain a pregnancy. When she again became pregnant, she was afraid to pin her hopes on carrying to full term. The long ordeal was emotionally draining, and she felt unable to face another attempt should this fail. I prayed the baby would thrive, even asking for a little girl to love; but in any case, I asked God to please give us a healthy child.

One early spring morning in 1999, my telephone rang. Upon answering it, I heard Beverly sobbing and stammering—she was losing this baby also, going through similar symptoms of miscarriage as before. We were both devastated! As I hung up the phone knowing how heartbroken she was and not being there to offer comfort, I was quite distressed. The realization we could be losing one more precious baby and never having another was heartbreaking.

Upon trudging upstairs and walking into the bathroom, my eyes were immediately drawn to a bird sitting on a bare tree branch close to the window. I was dumbfounded, as there, staring directly at me was a *bluebird*! There was no mistaking it!

It remained gazing at the window for a minute or so before taking flight. It gave me chills but also an understanding this was a subtle message from God that all would be well. Again, as in the dolphin sighting (see "A Harrowing Caribbean Adventure"), I knew this to be a spiritual blessing.

Immediately, I rushed to the phone to share this beautiful gift, which had just been offered. As far as I was concerned, there was no doubt my elusive little bluebird carried a message of sustained hope. There were still difficult days ahead, but I continued to have great faith in the message, and on August 24, 1999, my healthy and most precious little granddaughter, Madelyn Mary, was born.

There was a time in my life when I would not have recognized this as a communication from God. It would have been just another bird sitting on a tree branch. But since I have such a personal connection with bluebirds, it became something much more, and I was able to discern God speaking to me through His tiny creation. When we open ourselves up to an awareness of the unseen spiritual world surrounding us, we learn to trust more fully in God's love and concern for our well-being.

> *This is My Father's World*
> *And to My Listening Ears*
> *All Nature Sings and Round Me Rings*
> *The Music of the Spheres.*
> —*Maltbie Babcock,*
> *Christian hymn (1901)*

The Hidden Garden

In "The Power of Faith," which precedes this narrative, I related my experience of moving from Connecticut back to my home state of Pennsylvania and the remarkably lovely property God provided for my comfort and enjoyment. It was my home for three amazingly wonderful years.

Now, however, the property had been sold; and I needed to make other arrangements. *Where could I ever find a place that would equal this?* I couldn't... but God could! So, again, I prayerfully gave him my wish list. This time around, I asked for a home with the same peaceful qualities and beautiful surroundings, but in addition, I wanted a lot of windows, as the carriage house had been rather dark and I needed light! I had total faith God would hear my prayer again, as he had in 1997.

But now, I was only two weeks from moving, and getting anxious. I thought, *Why hadn't anything come along? Why wasn't my prayer being answered?* Previously, I had responded to a classified ad which sounded hopeful but heard nothing in response. Finally, however, I received a telephone reply from the property owner who lived out of state.

"Is there a garden?" I asked. "I need a place for a garden."

Being a bit fussy, I thought, *for someone who is two weeks away from a move with no place to go.*

However, the prospective landlady seemed quite nice and eagerly told me I could garden anywhere on the property.

"I also have a cat who goes where I go, and the ad says no pets," I stated. I cringed, afraid of the answer!

You're really pushing it, I thought!

"Oh, we love cats, just no dogs," she countered.

"Well then," I replied, "I'd like to take a look at it."

When I viewed the apartment on a bleak February day, I felt dejected. What a comedown! These quarters were much smaller than the carriage house I was vacating, with a tiny kitchen and very little storage space. Still, I especially liked one room which was encircled by windows on three sides, evoking the sensation of living in a tree house.

Perhaps this is *the place God has chosen for me*, I thought. *But it certainly doesn't measure up to what I had.*

The large property itself was sorely in need of some TLC. In addition to piles of trash that were scattered about, there were hundreds of dead branches and the ground was matted with leaves that hadn't seen a rake for years. It was more than depressing. But the house itself was wonderful—an old rambling English cottage in which the apartment was located.

Nevertheless, it was definitely a step down, and it made me despondent.

Why is God bringing me here? But the price was right, and I needed something quickly, so…

"I'll take it."

As spring approached, I was beginning to settle in but determined I could not live with the condition of the lawn and began to rake the leaves outside my door. But I couldn't stop there—it became an obsession to clean up the grounds, which were extensive. It was good outdoor exercise, and I enjoyed seeing the positive changes in the property.

And then, during the extensive cleanup, beneath a thick tangle of old wisteria vine and matted leaves, I uncovered a large terrace made from sizable granite blocks, at the edge of which were the old gardens lined with brick. How wonderful was this? It felt as though I was starring in a magical fairytale taken from an old storybook.

An inquiry revealed the home was built in the early 1950s by a woman who was an avid gardener. It was she who planted the enormous old trees now enveloping the property and the wisteria overhanging the huge yews surrounding the garden. The garden itself was a sunny and a warm-sheltered oasis of now-forgotten beauty. But that could be fixed!

As the weather warmed, each day I would see more evidence of her accomplishment—the iris was still there and the yarrow was peeking through. I cherished each plant emerging from the undergrowth that had covered it for so many years. Then and there, I resolutely determined to recreate the gardens as a tribute to this woman who had originated it, nurtured it until her death, and loved it enough to have her ashes spread on the grounds.

It became a spiritual mission, and as I gradually uncovered the beauty of her onetime property, I found myself becoming actually quite fond of my new home, until one day I was able to say, "You know what? I really love this place! Thank you for this blessing, God."

My experiences through the years have taught me to rely on Him for my needs. At the beginning of each new day, I try to place myself in His hands, depending on Him completely to fulfill the following promise He made:

Trust in the Lord with all thine heart; and lean not unto thine own understanding. In all thy ways acknowledge Him and He shall direct thy paths.
—Proverbs 3:5–6

There's a Bluebird on My Windowsill

Oh, the woes of getting on in years! In 2003, due to my family history of heart disease, I felt it might be worthwhile to undergo a heart stress test to which my general practitioner readily agreed. When the results came back, he told me everything was fine, except there was a slight abnormality and suggested I consult a cardiologist.

I had no apprehension whatsoever, but I did schedule an appointment with a cardiologist who told me point blank that everything was *not* fine and the *slight* abnormality was a partial blockage of the main artery going to my heart. He felt in order to correct this, I should start taking a prescription drug to reduce my cholesterol and schedule an angioplasty procedure which he would perform at the local hospital. I was not pleased with the solution he offered. And I certainly did not want to schedule surgery without looking at other options first.

The doctor was not happy when I told him I wanted to try my own approach to the problem. He correctly felt this was a risky path to take. I didn't blame him for feeling unsettled about my decision to put it off. However, he agreed to give me three months, at which time he would retest to reevaluate the situation. At no time did I feel concern but was very calm about receiving the diagnosis.

When I returned to my car and turned on the ignition, music was playing on the radio. The first words to reach my ears were song lyrics: *"There's a bluebird on your windowsill, there's a rainbow in your sky."* Since I have such a strong connection with bluebirds and look upon them as a portent of good fortune, I immediately knew this was a sign all would be well.

I need to disgress for a moment to explain I have never been a fan of prescription drugs. On the other hand, natural remedies have always fascinated me and given the choice I will always choose that option. In this case, however, I wasn't sure that was possible.

Then I recalled a weekly call-in radio program to which I had listened touting the use of their brand Omega-3 Fish Oil and Red Yeast Rice to lower cholesterol. All the callers sounded extremely positive regarding these products and reported great benefits to their health from taking them. Hmm! This seemed like a possible option.

So, during the next few months I faithfully took natural supplements of their brand Omega-3 Fish Oil and Red Yeast Rice. In addition, I increased my exercise and made a determined effort to be more careful regarding my diet, eliminating some unhealthy things and adding other more nutritionally sound food. It wasn't easy to do, but basically, I undertook a complete lifestyle change, although I must confess to cheating on occasion.

Upon returning to the hospital for retesting, the radiation stress test showed no sign of the blockage I had previously. In addition, a new blood test revealed my bad cholesterol numbers had dropped significantly while my good cholesterol had risen. Even now, many years later, everything continues to be normal. However, that is only because of being faithful to the healthy regimen I began back in 2003 and to which I remain faithful even now.

I find it beyond interesting the bluebird song was playing on the radio at the *exact* moment I needed to hear it. Do you agree?

A bluebird on my windowsill?

A rainbow in my sky?

That's good enough for me! I'll take it!

> *You may trust the Lord too little,*
> *but you can never trust Him too much.*
>
> —*Anonymous*

A Message from Beyond

My friend, Frieda, passed away suddenly on July 30, 2005, at the age of ninety-seven years. Her body was found outside in her beloved garden where, when not on her tractor mowing the lawn or gardening, she treasured time spent sitting under a shady tree during pleasant weather. Frieda was an amazing woman who would not let age diminish her participation in life.

The unexpected news raised goosebumps since we had discussed her future many times. She shared her concern of being forced to leave the home built by her husband and herself when young. A large property with a beautiful pond and her well-maintained gardens—it was the joy of her life. She loved her place dearly and could not be coaxed away, even for an overnight trip. So I told her my prayer was she would come to a peaceful end outside in the garden she loved. And she did! What a wonderful life she had… and what a perfect death! I was truly thrilled for her.

So for her funeral services, I decided to wear something bright and cheerful. No black would do for *this* funeral! From my closet, I chose a bright-blue jumper, with white flowers embroidered across the front, together with a floral pin she had given me. I decided against sending flowers being short of cash, having just left my job, and knew she would say "Don't do it." I had brought her flowers while she was alive, and I thought she would understand. However, I couldn't help feeling rather guilty.

As I spoke with people at the service, Dawn, a mutual friend of ours, told me she had seen her two days before her death. Frieda had leaned over the fence at the back of her property and waved and waved as Dawn stood outside the shop where she worked. Dawn said she continued waving back to her for the longest time before returning inside. Looking back, that seemed a pretty meaningful experience. I was somewhat jealous, since I hadn't seen Frieda for a couple weeks, and did not really get to say goodbye.

Frieda had carefully planned every aspect of her funeral, leaving explicit instructions as to what should take place. At the end of the graveside ceremony, each attendee was given an envelope containing a lovely card, on the front of which was a photograph of Frieda and a sentimental poem, above which was written "Frieda asked that these words be shared with you today." The inside of the card contained her name with the words:

> Here with us
> June 1, 1908–July 30, 2005

A little poem was written above, which I read aloud to a friend standing next to me:

> Don't go and buy a large bouquet
> For which you'll find it hard to pay.
> Don't stand around me looking blue;
> I may be better off than you!

We laughed! The humor was so much hers, and I thought very appropriate for me, in particular.

As we stood chatting at the gravesite, I noticed everyone else's card seemed to have a different poem than mine. Instead of being only four lines, the other cards contained a first verse which, upon examination, held no direct meaning for me. My particular card appeared to be the only one with a misprinted message.

Frieda's niece was quite apologetic and offered to get me a "better" one. But I emphatically said, "Absolutely not. It's a parting message to me from Frieda. I was meant to have this one."

Well, I had gotten my goodbye—except it wasn't really goodbye! God bless you, Frieda. You are indeed still here with us.

Always in my Heart.

Was This a Subconscious Premonition?

My daughter, Pattie, has been a member of Swan Creek Rowing Club in Lambertville, New Jersey, for many, many years. Each spring the beginning of rowing season on the Delaware River carries with it excitement and anticipation for all the rowers. She loves not only the exercise but the camaraderie with her fellow crew members.

On Palm Sunday 2006, she and Stella—another experienced club member—took a two-man shell onto the river from the club boat launch. They rowed quite a distance north then made the turn to come back when Pattie told Stella she thought they should review procedures to follow in case the boat flipped. So they went over exactly what should be done in the unlikely event this ever happened. This was highly unusual, as in all their years rowing, flipping the boat had never been discussed.

They proceeded downriver past the boat launch and started their turn to come back.

As they did so, Stella said, "This would be the absolute worst place to flip," since they were approaching the treacherous wing dam.

No sooner was the sentence spoken, when Pattie saw the bolts from her oarlock flying through the air as it came apart. Immediately, the boat overturned, and they suddenly found themselves submerged in bone-chilling fifty-two-de-

71

gree water, hanging onto the side of their shell as much as possible.

There was nobody in the immediate area to witness their predicament, but they finally caught the attention of two fishermen upstream in another boat by their frantic yells for help. However, since they were so close to the wing dam, a rescue attempt was dangerous and difficult. The fishermen finally managed to pull an exhausted Stella into their boat, but Pattie's rescue took longer. When the EMTs were at last able to place her in the ambulance, she was borderline hypothermic.

Both girls, of course, were mystified by their inexplicable urge to review lifesaving procedures prior to the accident. They credit this timely "coincidence," together with their excellent physical condition, for being able to survive the ordeal without major physical harm.

But again, it raises the question, *Was this just an extraordinary "coincidence," or was there something else at play here?* Going back over all my strange experiences through the years, I'm entirely sure where my verdict lies!

> *There are no mistakes,*
> *No coincidence*
> *All events are blessings*
> *Given to us to learn from.*
> —*Elizabeth Kübler-Ross*

Instant Gratification

One extremely rainy day in February 2008, while driving a major four-lane highway home from my daughter Barbara's in New Jersey, I not only heard but felt heavy road debris hit the undercarriage of my car. Within minutes, I was driving on a severely flattened front tire in the midst of a heavy downpour. This was not good! This was so far from good!

There was extremely heavy traffic and no shoulder that would suffice to pull off the highway. I was quite aware of smoke billowing up from the right front wheel, which was extremely scary; but there was nothing to be done except keep driving in this horrendous condition until I arrived at the next exit, a couple miles away.

When I finally managed to get off the highway onto an exit ramp, I straight away called for roadside assistance. They answered immediately, but the dispatcher advised it would be approximately forty-five minutes until someone could come to my rescue. Not what I wanted to hear! As traffic whizzed by, spraying me with water, I dejectedly ended the call.

Standing outside the car as far from the roadway as possible, I realized I had neglected to say my morning mantra asking for God's protection. So, ignoring the deluge coming down around me, I prayed aloud for God's help in this disturbing situation. Within minutes, my cell phone rang. Upon answering, I heard the tow truck driver saying he was coming up behind me. Oh, what happiness and relief to receive such comforting news! My hero!

After securing my car to his large flatbed truck, we went roaring off to the car dealership for repair. I commented on the quickness of his response, as I had been given a forty-five-minute dispatch time. Seems he was only two miles away when his dispatcher called with a cancellation. A quick U-turn, and he was on the scene within *two* minutes.

Extremely good news at the auto dealership also. Replacement of the shredded tire would take care of the problem, as there was no damage to the wheel or surrounding area, which seemed a true miracle in itself.

Life has many lessons to teach us, if we would only listen. At a time of desperation, a worried, distraught woman sent an emotional prayer to God. He responded quickly and decisively. Lesson Learned!

God answers Prayer.

Communication Has Been Shut Off

Arnie was an email friend with whom I had been communicating regarding our mutual interest in the ancestry of our forebears in Baltimore, Maryland.

Much correspondence had been sent back and forth between us for well over a year. Such a blessing to have a convenient way of communicating, being so much faster and easier than going through the snail mail of the post office. I always looked forward to hearing from him with news of a new find or anything of interest regarding this family. I'm certain he felt the same; consequently, we were faithful correspondents.

One morning, I opened an email from Arnie, telling me he was going into the hospital for heart surgery, so I didn't expect to hear from him for a period of time. When he did get in touch at some point following his operation, he confided he wasn't feeling great and had some upcoming doctors' visits scheduled. He was fervently hoping they could help him gain more energy and motivation.

On Friday, February 8 at 6:15 p.m., I dashed off an email inquiring about his health since seeing his doctors. He replied later that evening at 10:48 p.m. saying they had cut down his meds and he was gaining strength with each day. More than anything, he was anxious to return to genealogy.

When I read that latest email response on Saturday morning, February 9, I immediately sent a reply at 8:42 a.m.

telling him how happy I was to hear the good news; I had missed him. At 9:04 a.m., I received an email message from the postmaster saying delivery had failed. How odd! So, I sent a completely new message at 9:30 a.m. Again, a postmaster return—delivery had failed. Too strange!

Since I suspected a problem with his computer, I contacted him by phone to tell him of the issue. When I placed the call, his wife answered, and I began telling her of my attempt to reach her husband by email without success. Gasping for breath, she tearfully interjected he had passed away that morning after stepping out of the shower. Oh my dear god! How shocking!

After expressing my deepest sympathy and profusely apologizing for calling at such a critical time, I hung up the phone and immediately made the mental connection between the messages I had received from the postmaster and Arnie's passing. "Coincidence?" Oh, I think not!

I can say, with absolute certainty, Arnie, our emails on this earthly plane are finished; but my ardent hope is you've met our elusive ancestors in another dimension and know firsthand their story.

> *Synchronicity is an ever-present reality*
> *for those who have eyes to see it.*
>
> —*Carl Jung*

It's Not Luck, Brandon!

For quite a while, I had been toying with the idea of purchasing a gravesite in a lovely old tree-shaded cemetery located in my hometown of Hatboro where my parents and some of my ancestors are buried. I have a great affinity for old cemeteries in any case, but this particular burial ground has special meaning, since I went there quite a bit during my childhood. Memorial Day ceremonies and decorating the graves of my grandparents were traditional every year. Many of the surnames inscribed on the headstones are old and familiar families that I knew at one time or another through the years. Being a very nostalgic person, it holds a special place in my heart.

It had been a couple months since I telephoned the cemetery office inquiring as to availability of plots in section F where my parents are interred. At that time, I was informed only two remained unsold in that particular section. As a long-established procrastinator, I pretty much forgot about it until one day, in Hatboro on another errand, I wanted to put flowers on my parents' grave, which I did occasionally. After placing the flowers, I remembered my telephone call and wandered over to the office.

As I walked through the door, a young fellow who introduced himself as Brandon sauntered over to speak with me. After explaining my purpose, he readily said he would show me the two lots still available. As we walked to the site, he was checking the plot plan and simultaneously consulting someone on the telephone. Then he turned to tell me one had already been sold, but he said, "Let me show you the other one." He pointed! Following his gaze, the realization broke that the plot he was indicating was directly in front of and facing my parent's gravesite.

We were pretty amazed at the happy "coincidence," but I became curious as to the actual number of lots in the sector where mine was being purchased. Brandon incredulously informed me section F contained 270 lots overall.

As I was filling out paperwork in the office, Brandon said, "Boy, you were lucky!"

"It's not luck, Brandon!" I replied.

That lesson has taken me a lifetime to learn, but I think I've finally figured it out!

Coincidences are spiritual puns.
—*G. K. Chesterton*

PART III

Subconscious Communication with Our Ancestors?

A few of my out-of-the ordinary stories center around long deceased relatives, primarily while engaged in furthering the family genealogy which has served as a hobby, a needed diversion, and ardent passion over the years.

It goes without saying—we all have ancestors, or we certainly wouldn't be here. But the large majority of people take them for granted, giving them no thought whatsoever. My own interest was completely nonexistent in my younger days. Only after my elders departed this earth did my own curiosity became aroused.

Regrettably, the time had long passed to sit down over a cup of tea, ask questions, and listen to memories and stories of their earlier years. I'm filled with misgivings, but nothing can change that! Nevertheless, I try to give them life by delving into the history of their past, back through many generations. These are the kinfolk who preceded me on this earth and whose DNA is carried in my blood—my family!

We are blessed to be living at a time when testing for DNA is a simple process, thus providing us the capability of connecting with family, both contemporary and generations past. Also, we now have been given a means of defining our ethnicity. Where are our ancestors from? Are we European, African, Native American, Scandinavian, etc.? Exploring our DNA has become big business in recent years as more and more people become interested in pursuing their origins.

Native Americans have a strong belief in *blood memory*. I have seen this defined as a genetic connection to our forebears through spirituality, language, song, and teachings. There is most certainly an inherent connection with our ancestors, if only through the DNA in our white blood cells. But is it more than that?

I have spent many pleasurable hours researching my family, but while so doing, odd and unusual (almost spooky) occurrences have raised thoughtful questions in my mind. Yes, some of them are funny "coincidences," but is that the complete story? Or is it possible our deceased ancestors still have a connection with us through time and space? It certainly has made me wonder, and reading through the next few stories may make you wonder also!

Researching Our Ancestors— Guided by Spirit

I have always felt a certain closeness to the ancestors I am researching, which I attribute partly to being a lover of history. As such, I enjoy imagining these folks going about their daily routine, dressed in the old-fashioned attire of the time period in which they lived. For me, not only is the quest to locate the ancestor but to identify the actual property where they resided and other countless details which make them seem more alive in my mind's eye.

The following incident, however, has nothing to do with imagination; it happened, and it happened exactly as I now tell it!

When I awoke the morning of August 5, 1998, I vaguely recalled a dream, and although the particulars of the dream were not vivid, standing out very clearly in my mind was the message from the dream—"I needed a challenge." As I lay there thinking about that, I decided since I had nothing to do that day, I would challenge myself to drive to Norristown, Pennsylvania, to visit the Montgomery County Archives and the Historical Society of Montgomery County.

For me, this was a formidable task and something I had been putting off for months, since I have a fear of driving to unfamiliar places and being unsure where I am going.

However, I decided to attempt it. I was successful and arrived at the archives at about 10:00 a.m.

The archives keep records of marriage licenses from 1885 and old wills and deeds. Montgomery County split off from Philadelphia County in 1784, so any information prior to that date is usually found in Philadelphia County records. However, I was fortunate to locate an early deed for my family's property in Gwynedd, Pennsylvania, which was dated 1772 but for some reason, not recorded until 1905. A good start to my day, but it was about to get better.

While at the archives, two ladies entered, and I overheard them say they were from Illinois and were searching for a family named *Major*. The three of us were the only researchers at the archives during my time there.

Upon completing my research, I moved on to the Historical Society of Montgomery County a few blocks away. As I sat looking through a large book of records from Abington Presbyterian Church gathering information regarding my grandmother's family—the *Lockards*—of Abington and Cheltenham Townships, the two ladies I had seen previously entered. As they walked over to my area with the librarian, I heard them mention the Abington Presbyterian Church. I looked up in astonishment!

They were relating to the librarian their Major family lived in Gwynedd in the 1700s and attended the Abington Presbyterian Church, which is a few miles from Gwynedd. I was quite taken aback and turned to tell them I was using that book as I had family in Abington, but in addition, I had other family in Gwynedd during the same time period whose line I was also researching. This seemed so strange, and we remarked on the "coincidence."

When I finished using the book, I presented it to them and went to the card catalog to check for my family from

Gwynedd. While there, I also looked for *Major*, and since there were several cards, I mentioned this to the women. The three of us were the only researchers at this library also.

I busied myself with other research, and before long, one of the women walked over to thank me for pointing out the card file, as it led them to an article in an old scrapbook confirming property in Gwynedd belonging to their Major ancestor. Although they had been told this property existed, no deed or anything else pertaining to the land was ever found, even though they had been looking for several years.

The scrapbook mentioning the Major property in Gwynedd caught my attention as it was very old and worn, characteristics which, to me, make it highly interesting. I asked if I might look through it out of curiosity. The scrapbook was put together by a gentleman named Edward Matthews, and upon inspection, I found it contained old newspaper articles which appeared to chronicle sales of farm property.

After perusing a couple pages, I stumbled upon an article regarding a Doylestown Township, Bucks County, property which was referred to as the "Sumpstone Farm." It turned out to be the old Adam/John Frankenfield farm where my grandfather was shown to be living as a child of eleven years with his aunt and uncle (the John Frankenfields) in the 1860 census. The librarian was forbidden to photocopy from this fragile book, so I dashed off a few quick notes as it was closing time. I wrote down enough information to determine the property was located on the Edison-Furlong Road, approximately one mile from Easton Road in Doylestown Township.

The next day, still craving adventure, I was determined to locate the property. So from Easton Road, I turned onto Edison-Furlong, and when the odometer was approaching a mile, I quickly made a turn into a long gravel driveway that suddenly appeared on my left. I held my breath, hoping there would be an old farmhouse at the end of it. And there was!

I knocked at the door and explained my purpose to the woman who answered. She graciously invited me inside and showed me the original part of the house. I was pretty confident this was the Frankenfield home but not positive, even though the article stated a barn was situated east of the house, and there was one at that location.

She asked if the article mentioned an old tree, and I did remember such a reference. We went outside, and she pointed to a huge white oak that is 350–400 years old and designated a historic tree of Bucks County. I knew then without question—I had found it!

I had been searching for the specific location of this property in Bucks County but unable to pinpoint it. Then, to go to Montgomery County because of a dream and find it in a scrapbook I would never have noticed except for meeting two women from Illinois, who were there the same, *exact* time, had ancestors in the same, *exact* locations and during the same, *exact* time period is truly astounding!

There are forces at work in the universe we do not understand, and this convergence of circumstances seems too amazing to be explained away by "*coincidence.*"

But wait, there's more!

Upon reviewing the Gwynedd deeds in my possession, I found the forty-nine-acre property owned by my great-great-great-great-grandparents *John and Margaret Weeks* in 1788 was bounded on a property line by that of Alexander Major's land. They were neighbors, for heaven's sake!

It's kind of fun to think perhaps John Weeks and Alexander Major, from another dimension, were playing a role in guiding their descendants to discover the history of their families that lived in this area over two hundred years ago.

Old Adam/John Frankenfield home, Bucks County, PA

The Christmas Gift

Shortly before Christmas, I visited our old local cemetery to place wreaths upon the graves of my parents and grandparents which, through the years, has become more or less an annual tradition. I enjoy making the festive wreaths or sprays myself. Part of the seasonal fun was cutting and gathering evergreens then decorating them with acorns, pinecones, holly, and large, red bows—one of my great joys of the season!

This particular year, as I placed the greens on my grandparents' grave, I was silently talking to my grandmother Susan, telling her how unfortunate it was we never knew each other, as she died rather young, many years before I was born. There's always been a gentle touch of melancholy in my heart at not having known her—or any of my other grandparents, for that matter. Each grandparent was long gone before I came along. How sad!

Returning to the car, I noticed a red plastic poinsettia directly on the spot where I had to step to enter the automobile. I had not seen it previously, although it may have been there, but my immediate thought was, *It's a little gift from my grandmother*, and I lightly threw it on the passenger seat.

Upon returning home, I laid it on some Christmas greens I had placed on a shelf in my living room and gave it no more thought.

That year, my New Year's resolution was to bring my extensive genealogy research to some sort of completion and begin to write the family history. So, after the new year, I began sorting and organizing through many files accumulated for years during my ancestry quest. Of course, this resulted in finding bits and pieces of information which had been put aside for another day.

Some of my notes indicated there might be a Quaker line that needed a closer look on my grandmother Susan's side. I had not planned to do research but found it intriguing, as always, and began to explore. To make a very long story quite short, doors opened leading to a whole new Quaker family that extended back into the 1600s in America and answered many questions that for years remained unresolved. I was so happy I could burst!

As I put my Christmas decorations away for another year, it suddenly dawned on me the artificial poinsettia I found and placed on the greens was directly in front of various Scottish items placed there in tribute to my Scottish heritage through Grandmother Susan's paternal family. Was she speaking to me? Or was the entire incident that transpired merely "coincidence?" Perhaps. But then… *perhaps not!*

My fondest hope is that "Roots" may start black, white, brown, red, yellow people digging back for their own roots. Man, that would make me feel 90 feet tall.

—Alex Haley,
author of Roots

The Welcoming Spirit

At one time, many, many years ago, a small but charming antique shop was located in the historic building known as the Olde Shovel Shoppe in the village of Cheltenham, Pennsylvania. The building itself is a longstanding structure, the original section dating back to about 1774, with a later addition completed in the early 1800s. It is on both the National Register of Historic Places and the Pennsylvania Inventory of Historic Places.

My cousin Grace related to me an interesting little tale regarding this building involving her mother, Emma. As she tells it, Emma's close friend was an avid collector of antiques and asked Emma to accompany her to this picturesque little shop, a decision which proved most interesting! Upon entering the building, she felt herself surrounded with a warm, welcoming sense of belonging—she was supposed to be there. She had been invited!

Completely enamored with the building itself, she meandered off on her own to explore, much to the annoyance of the shop owner. But not to be deterred, she wandered through the dim hallways and was overcome with the sense of a strong female presence. Upon arriving home, she excitedly shared this experience with Grace. Captivated and totally bewildered, it was not until quite sometime later when she believed the answer to this unusual occurrence was finally revealed.

Driving through Cheltenham one day with her father, they were passing by the Olde Shovel Shoppe when her dad casually mentioned going there as a young child with his parents. He went on to explain that it had been the longtime residence of his grandparents, David and Mary Lockard.

Eureka! Here was a startling revelation formerly unknown to Emma. Immediately, she made the connection between her odd experience and this new piece of information. Now her previous feelings had some roots! It all began to make sense in a strange sort of way. Seemingly, she had been invited into this family home by a very hospitable, albeit deceased great-grandparent.

> *Signals from spirit may be elaborate or simple,*
> *but they are always around us.*
>
> —*James Van Praagh*

The Lockard family occupied the house known as the
Olde Shovel Shoppe, having moved into the residence
in 1885 and living there until at least 1910.

An April Fool's Joke

On April 1, 2003, I turned again to my favorite hobby, gene-alogy, which I had neglected for quite some time. My thought was to check the 1880 census to look for a daughter of my great-great-grandfather, Thomas Lockard of Cheltenham. In order to verify her correct name, which totally escaped me, I searched my files for a photograph of her father, as I recalled her name being inscribed on the back. Unable to locate it, I placed a telephone call to Betty, the church historian who had originally provided the photograph. We had become quite friendly, and I knew she would be delighted to double-check.

When she answered the phone and I told her who was calling, she said, "I can't believe it's you! I was just addressing an envelope to send you something."

Since I had no contact with her for well over a year, that seemed pretty "coincidental." She came across some-thing she thought might be useful in my research and passed along information from the Montgomery County Register of Wills, which someone had given her regarding my ances-tor William Lockard. She mentioned being occupied doing research for a member of the Dannehower family who, at one time, lived on Laurel Lane in Cheltenham. I was unfamiliar with the name.

After our conversation, looking through my list of records from Montgomery County where I record everything I've researched there, I picked up the deeds list. I located a record of a deed listing my ancestor William Lockard as grantee on property purchased from Jonas Dannehower. The land was located on Laurel Lane. Oh, for heaven's sake! They both sequentially owned the same property. Now, really!

I strongly suspect our deceased ancestors are tuned into our search and attempt to aid in the quest from another realm. This is not the first time something of this nature has happened while tracing my family, and other researchers have voiced the same thing.

I'm willing to concede it's highly unlikely William Lockard and Jonas Dannehower were playing an April fool's joke—much too wild and imaginative! But whatever it was, it got *my* attention that's for sure!

> *Coincidence is God's way*
> *of remaining anonymous.*
>
> *—Albert Einstein*

The Campbells Are Coming

When it became known to me John and Jane Campbell, my great-great-grandparents, were buried at Abington Friends Meeting, there was absolutely no question I was going to visit this longstanding site myself. John had died sometime after 1820 and Jane in 1851, so was it even possible to find the gravestones after so many years? Well, I was certainly about to find out!

Seeing the property upon arriving the first time, I was enamored by the Quaker simplicity and beauty of the surroundings. The focal point is the very old Quaker meeting house itself enveloped by large, towering trees. Timeworn cemeteries hold an enchantment for me anyway, but this was particularly charming.

I was pleased to find the office staffed and enlisted the assistance of Dave, the caretaker, who was extremely helpful. From a well-worn book of gravestone inscriptions, which were copied by Jennie C. Saunders in September 1932 (ironically, my birthday month and year), he determined there was a John Campbell, who died in 1826, next to a Jane Campbell.

Proceeding outside, Dave escorted me to the oldest section of the cemetery where he began to count off rows in the area where their gravesites were shown. However, it seemed the row we were looking for was missing. Oh no! In addition, stones that had survived were almost illegible.

We were just about to give up when, looking down, I saw the letters *mpbell* staring up at me from atop the gravestone directly below me. Closer examination proved it was indeed a Campbell grave. From the tombstone immediately adjacent, Dave was able to make out the word *Jane*. I was thrilled and likewise Dave. He explained how relatively rare it is to identify these weathered, old stones.

We took several photos, and after thanking Dave profusely, I began my journey home. I felt happy and excited, like a real winner! As I started north on the main road, a small, white truck appeared immediately ahead of me with a name boldly emblazoned on the back, in large black letters, "Campbell Electric." This was not something you could miss. What were the chances? I continued following the truck for quite a few miles, just cracking up at the irony.

Addendum: I was rewriting diligently to bring the above Campbell story to completion for this book, but it was late at night; I was not at my best. Turning off the computer, I mentally told myself I would think about it the following day.

The next morning, upon turning on my computer, I noticed an email from another Campbell researcher. Our great grandmothers, Charlotte and Elizabeth Campbell, were sisters in the mid-1800's. We had not communicated for nine months, but there she was—reaching out for assistance with our Campbell ancestry *at just that moment in time.*

This delightful little story has now turned into a chronicle with a surplus of "coincidental" happenings, even discounting the book of inscriptions penned on my birth date. Too bizarre! What is this craziness? I want to believe the spirits of my ancestors are letting me know they are still around. But there are no apparent answers in our finite world. However, it does indeed make you wonder!

> *We are linked by blood, and blood is*
> *memory without language.*
> —*Joyce Carol Oates*

Epilogue

Finally, springtime has come to our part of the country. It was a long time arriving this year, but now, it's early May—my favorite month! I count myself blessed to sit here at my large front window gazing upon a serene background filled with blossoming trees and a landscape dotted with colorful tulips and daffodils. Outside my window, I glimpse a winding path through the greenery next to which a gazebo invites the walker to sit and rest awhile. How lovely!

If I strolled through my open door, I would be standing on a spacious front porch filled with nostalgic old furniture, some of which has followed me from home to home throughout my lifetime. A very worn bench which creates a summer home for my indoor plants was used by my mother to hold her laundry basket as she hung her wet clothes out to dry so long ago. I'm *so* sentimental. Should I choose to pick a flower or two, my garden lies directly in front. And I only need to stoop down and dig in the good, rich soil to scatter seeds that will give me and my neighbors much pleasure and enjoyment through the coming summer months.

This lovely little cottage is located on the grounds of a longstanding Quaker retirement community, which is a little gem hidden away in a historic old town in Bucks County, Pennsylvania. It is small, the staff is caring, and the residents feel like family. It's idyllic and much more than I ever could have hoped for. God brought me here!

This is a place where I can still count myself as useful to others. I have been blessed with extremely good health, but there are many here not so fortunate. Perhaps I can be helpful to them. It gives purpose to my life, makes me feel good, and fulfills God's instruction, "Do unto others"!

This could very well be the last stopover on my life's path. If so, that's okay! I have learned much on this journey, mostly due to the innumerable spiritual experiences with which God has seen fit to bless me. By far, the greatest lesson I've learned, however, is not to be afraid of death. No fear!

As I've said again and again, there is so very much more to our existence than what can be seen and touched on this earth. When the time comes, I will welcome death as a friend, trusting in the words of our Lord:

Yea, though I walk through the valley of the shadow
of death, I will fear no evil for Thou art with me.
—Psalms 23:4 (KJV)

Every Man's Life Is a

Fairy Tale

Written by

God's Fingers

In which the end
is really the beginning...

Hans Christian Anderson

About the Author

The author presently lives in Bucks County, Pennsylvania, with—until recently—her calico kitty, Madeline. She raised three accomplished daughters and has lived to see five grandchildren and four great-grandchildren. An avid gardener, cat lover, long-time genealogist, and devotee of time-honored, traditional Christian hymns, this is her first book.